First Facts

DATA MANIA

Lions and Tigers and Graphs! Oh My!

by Jennifer M. Besel

Consultant:
Michele Koomen, PhD
Co-Chair and Assistant Professor of Education
Gustavus Adolphus College
St. Peter, Minnesota

CAPSTONE PRESS
a capstone imprint

First Facts is published by Capstone Press,
151 Good Counsel Drive, P.O. Box 669, Mankato, Minnesota 56002.
www.capstonepub.com

Printed in the United States of America in North Mankato, Minnesota.
082011
006231CGVMI

Books published by Capstone Press are manufactured with paper containing at least 10 percent post-consumer waste.

Library of Congress Cataloging-in-Publication Data
Besel, Jennifer M.
Lions and tigers and graphs! Oh my! / by Jennifer M. Besel.
p. cm.—(First facts. Data mania)
Summary: "Uses animals in a zoo to explore how using graphs can help readers organize and understand information"—Provided by publisher.
Includes bibliographical references and index.
ISBN 978-1-4296-4527-0 (library binding)
ISBN 978-1-4296-6341-0 (paperback)
1. Mathematical statistics—Graphic methods—Juvenile literature. I. Title. II. Series.

QA276.13.B47 2011
001.4'226—dc22 2010000549

Editorial Credits
Christopher L. Harbo, editor; Matt Bruning, designer and illustrator; Eric Mankse, production specialist

Photo Credits
Alamy/blickwinkel, 9 (tiger)
iStockphoto/Carlos Andres, cover, 9 (chalkboard); Ivan Cholakov, 21 (monkey); Jamie Carroll, 13 (penguin); Jonathan Heger, 9 (lion); Jonathan Livingston, 17; Nikolay Suslov, 12 (fish); Stilyan Savov, background (throughout)
Shutterstock/Andrejs Jegorovs, 7 (zebra); Artem Illarionov, 7 (sitting bear); Danny Smythe, 12 (bucket); Eric Gevaert, 21 (baboon); Eric Isselée, 7 (standing zebra); Juan David Ferrando Subero, 5 (fence); mylifeiscamp, 7 (bear); nachogalacho, 5 (sign); Nitr, 15; Richard A. McGuirk, 13 (seal); Schalke fotografie/Melissa Schalke, 13 (dolphin); Serg64, 5 (sky)

Table of Contents

Seeing Information

Look! Can you see the animals? Oops. You're not tall enough to see over the fences at the zoo. Well, good thing we have graphs. With graphs, you can see lots of information at one time. No long necks required. Come on! I'll show you.

A graph is like a picture book. It tells a story about how much there is or how many there are of something. Graphs can also tell you how something changed.
This way to Data Zoo

Picture This

On a **pictograph**, small pictures show big things. I drew 10 bears on the top row of my zoo pictograph. I drew 10 because there are 10 bears in the zoo. In the second row, I drew seven zebras. Now look at the graph. See? The zoo has more bears than zebras.

pictograph—a graph that uses pictures to show how many there are of something

Bears and Zebras at the Zoo

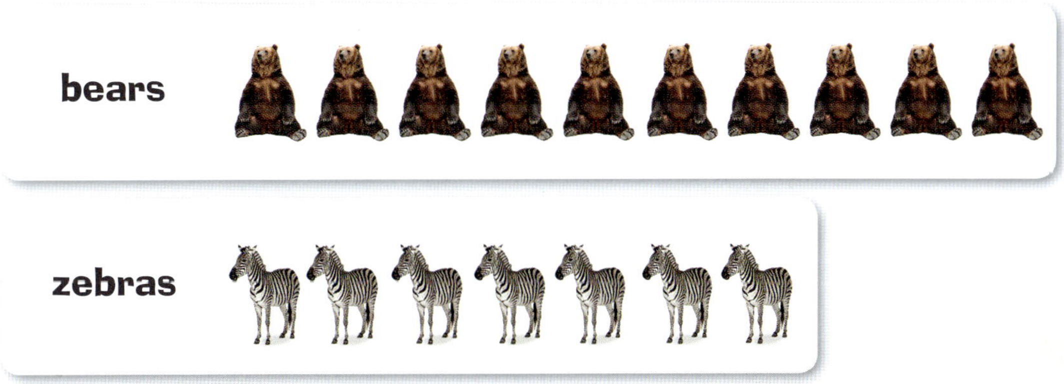

1 picture = 1 animal

Counting the Tallies

The tiger and lion raced nine times to see which one was faster. I used a **tally** chart to keep track of the races. Tally charts are great for counting things as they happen. After each race, I drew a line next to the winner's name. At the end, I counted the tally marks. Look at the graph to see which animal won.

tally—a mark made to keep track of a score or record

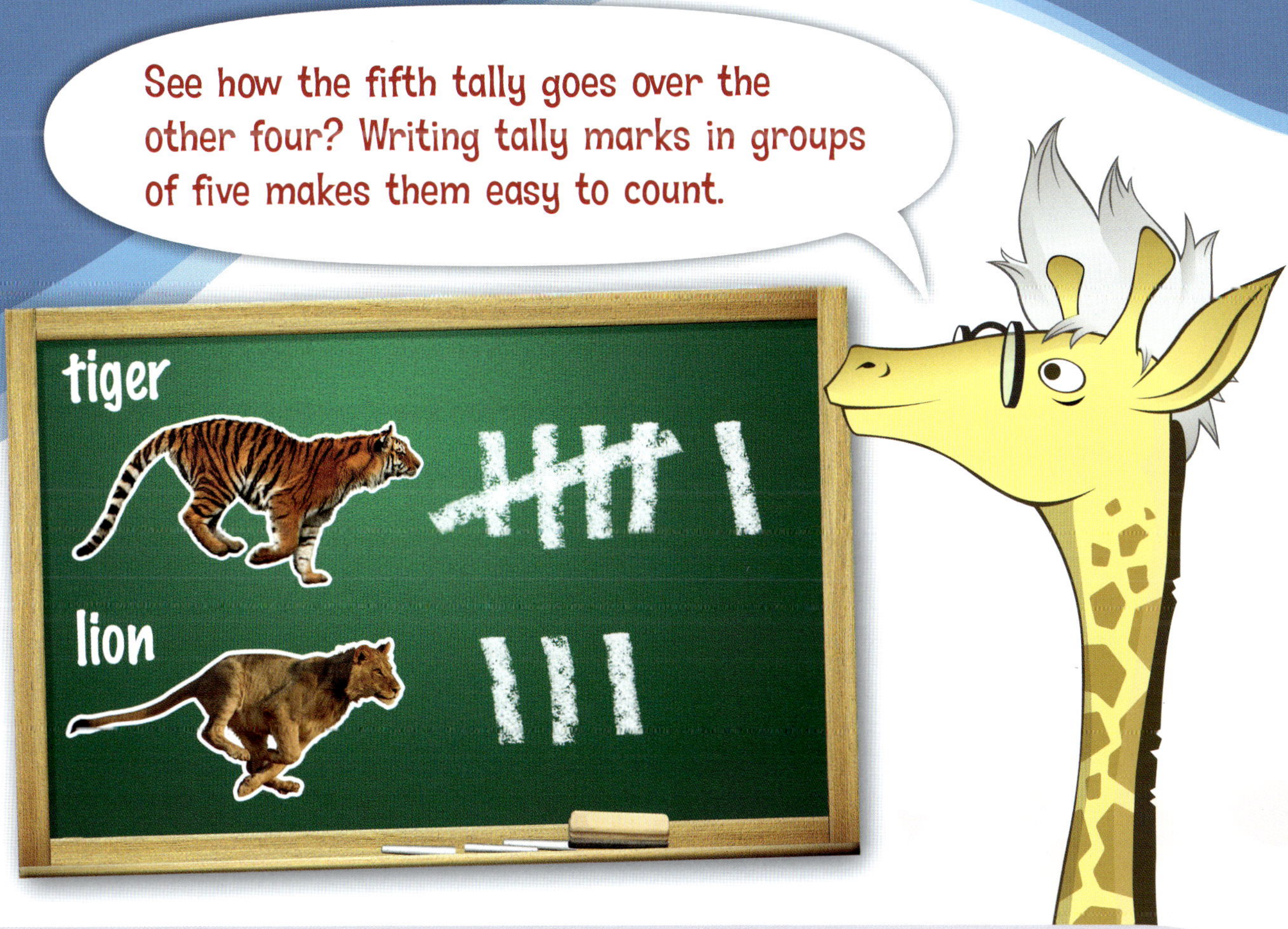

Choosing a Story

Graphs tell only one story at a time. For example, the tally chart shows which cat won the most races. But it doesn't show how big those animals are or what they eat. When you make a graph, you have to choose a story to tell. If you need to tell another story, you have to make another graph. But that's OK! Who doesn't love making graphs?

Setting the Bar

Bar graphs **compare** things without pictures. The zookeeper says I'm the tallest land animal. I made a bar graph to see if she's right.

On the left side of the paper, I wrote numbers for the heights. This part is the graph's y-**axis**. Across the bottom, or x-axis, are the names of animals we'll compare. Then I drew a bar for each animal. I am 14 feet tall. So the bar reaches the number 14. The taller the animal, the taller the bar.

Heights of Land Animals

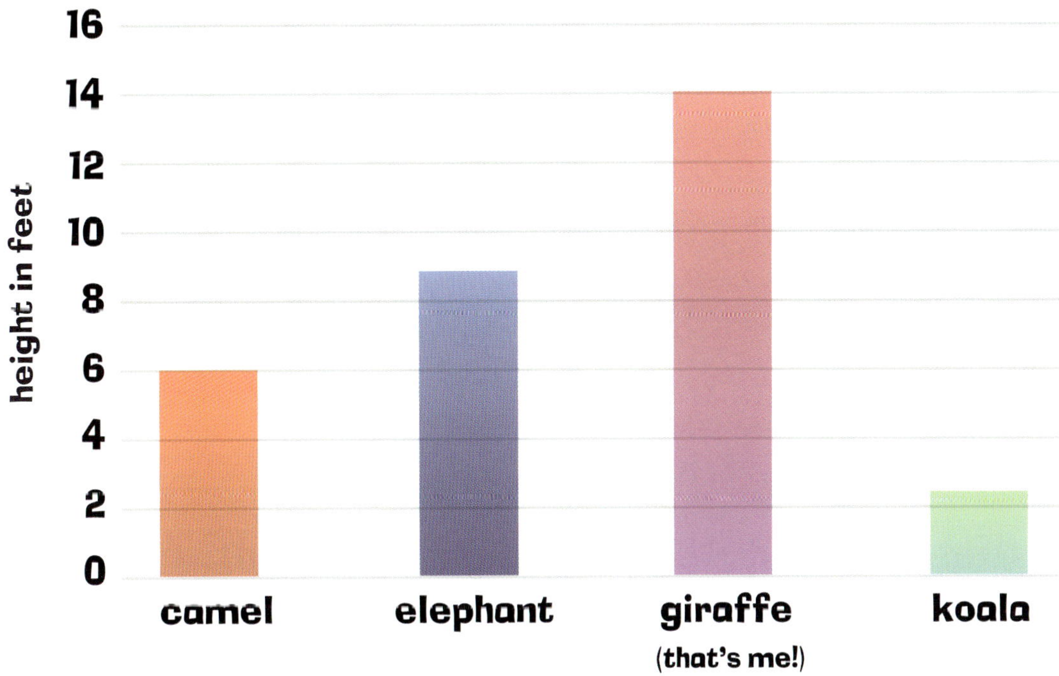

compare—to judge one thing against another and note similarities and differences

axis—a line at the side or bottom of a graph

Zookeepers serve a lot of slippery fish for lunch. The zoo's bar graph shows which animal eats the most fish.

Some bar graphs go up and down. Others go side to side. On the zoo's bar graph, the bigger the number, the longer the bar. How many pounds of fish did the dolphin eat? If you said 20 pounds, you are correct! Easy as pie.

The title of a graph is like a secret clue. It tells you what information you'll find in the graph.

Who Eats the Most Fish?

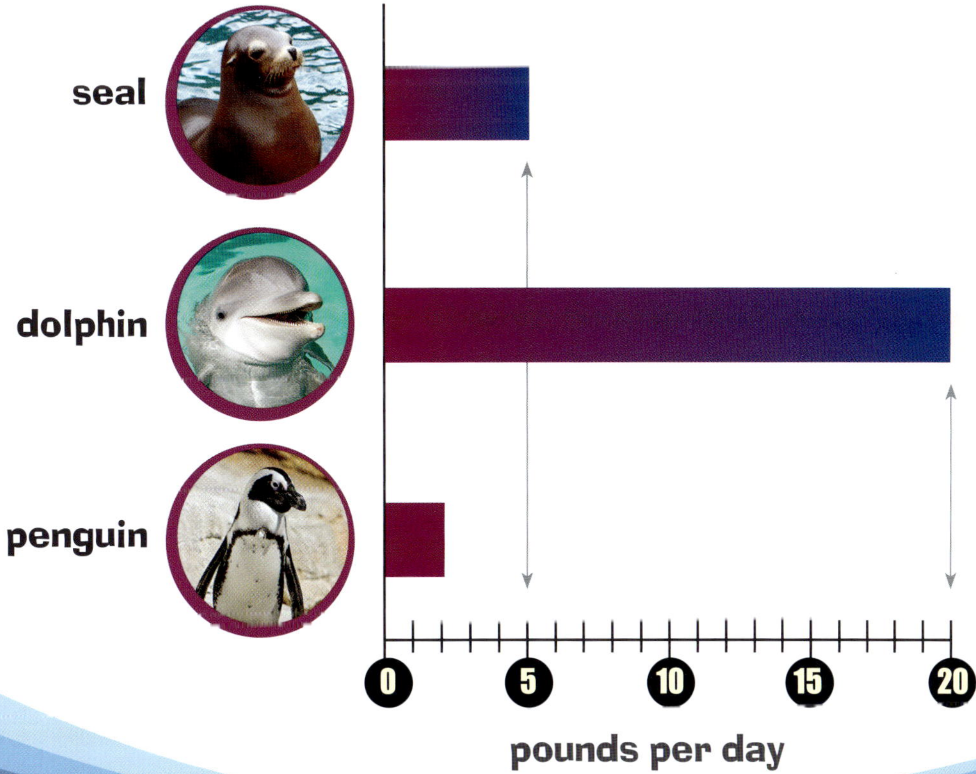

Data Pies

Speaking of pie, there's a graph called a pie chart. No, it's not made of pie! Pie charts are also called circle graphs. The circle stands for an entire group of something. In my graph, the circle stands for all the snacks I ate last week.

The circle is cut into pieces. Each piece stands for one day. I ate apples three days last week. So three pieces on the graph are red. There are more red pieces on the graph than anything else. I do love apples!

My Snacks

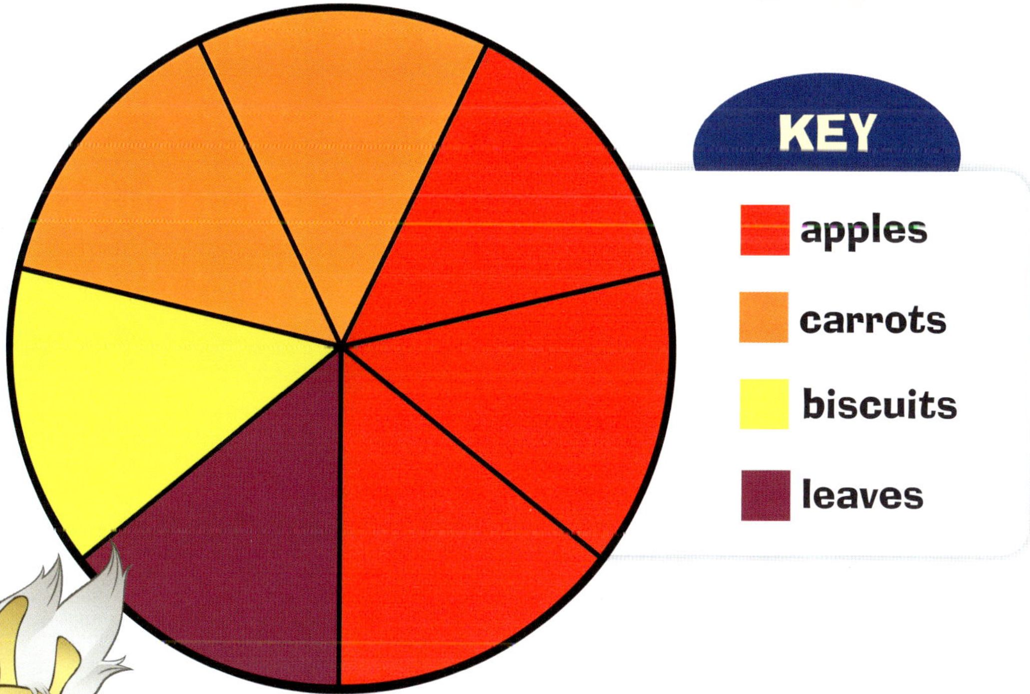

KEY
apples
carrots
biscuits
leaves

See that box by the graph? That's the key. The key tells you what each color in the pie chart stands for.

Here we are at the flamingo pond. I took a **poll** of my feathered friends to see how they spend their days. Check out my pie chart to see the results.

How many flamingos answered the poll? If you need a clue, count the number of slices in the pie. What did the flamingos do the least often? If you said go swimming, you're right!

poll—a survey of opinions

Flamingos' Favorite Things to Do

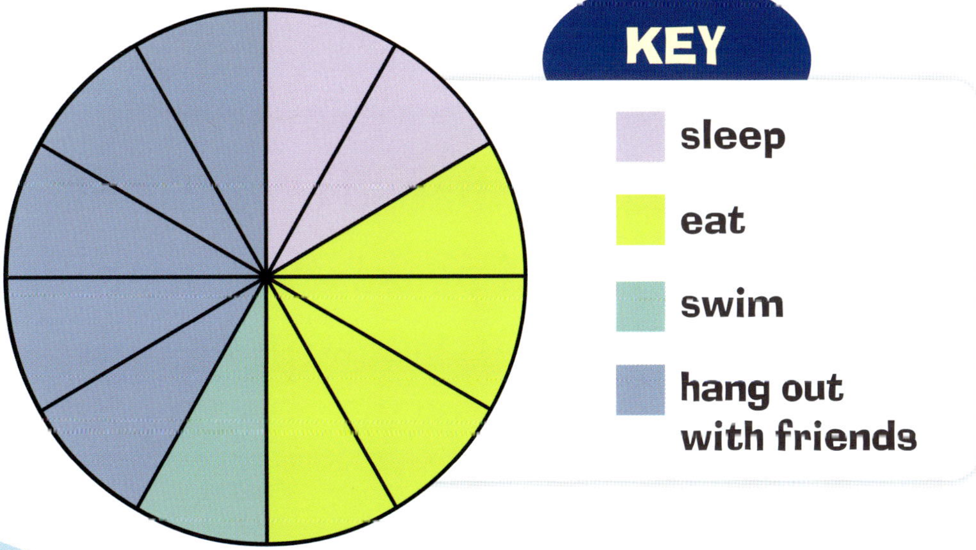

Lining Up a Graph

The last graph we'll monkey around with is the line graph. Line graphs show how something changed over time. When you look at a line graph, you'll see lines that aren't straight. The parts of a line that go down are called valleys. The parts that go up are called peaks. Valleys and peaks show that a change happened. When the line is flat, there was no change.

Peaks and Valleys

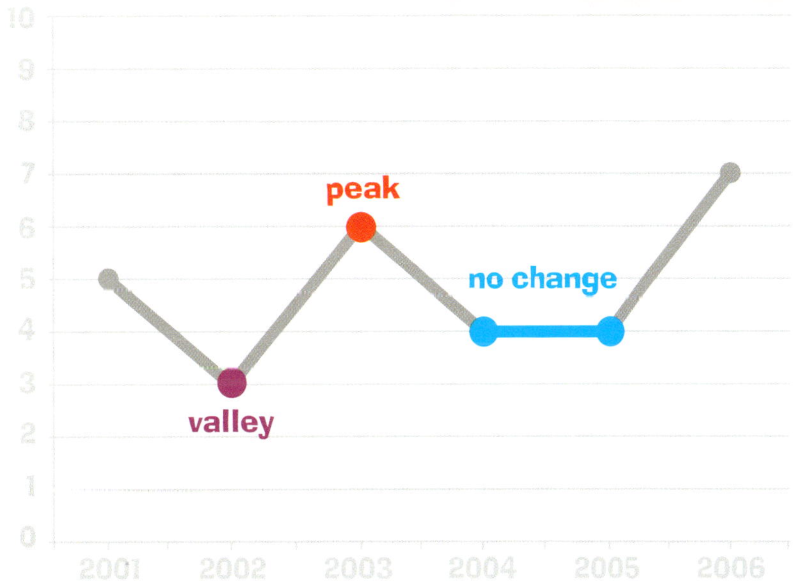

How Do You Choose Which Graph to Use?

Graphs are like superheroes. They each have a special power. Look at this handy chart to choose the super graph you need.

- Line graphs—show changes over time
- Pie charts—show differences within a whole group
- Pictographs and bar graphs—compare amounts of things
- Tally charts—count things as they happen

Zookeepers used a line graph to see changes in the monkey **population**. The x-axis shows the years being compared. The y-axis shows the number of monkeys. In 2000, 16 spider monkeys lived at the zoo. From 2006 to 2008, the baboon population really grew.

Now you know how to see lots of information without a long neck. Graphs are amazing! Go graph your world today.

population—the total number of animals that live in a place

Monkey Population 2000 - 2010

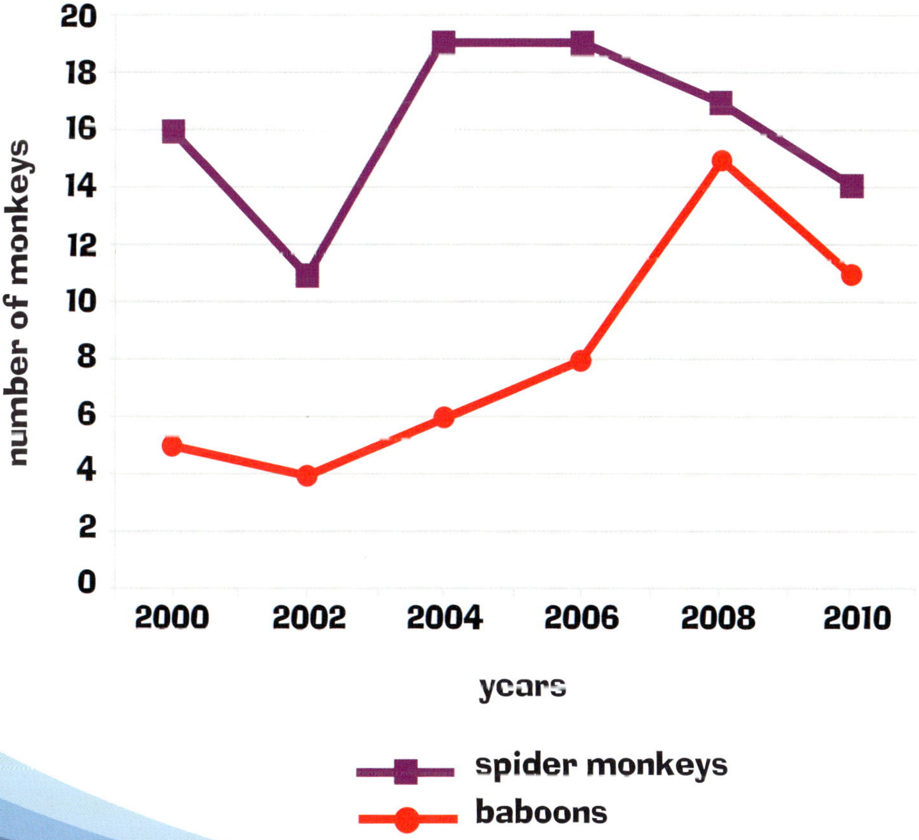

Glossary

axis (AK-sis)—a line at the side or bottom of a graph

compare (kuhm-PAIR)—to judge one thing against another and note similarities and differences

pictograph (PIK-toh-graf)—a graph that uses pictures to show how many there are of something; sometimes this graph is called a picture graph

poll (POHL)—a survey of opinions or beliefs

population (pop-yuh-LAY-shun)—the total number of people or animals that live in a place

tally (TAL-ee)—a mark made to keep track of a score or record

Read More

Marrewa, Jennifer. *Graphing Favorite Things.* Math in Our World. Pleasantville, N.Y.: Weekly Reader Publishing, 2008.

Piddock, Claire. *Line, Bar, and Circle Graphs.* My Path to Math. New York: Crabtree, 2010.

Underwood, Deborah. *Safari Adventure: Charts, Graphs, and Tables.* Raintree Fusion. Chicago: Raintree, 2008.

Internet Sites

FactHound offers a safe, fun way to find Internet sites related to this book. All of the sites on FactHound have been researched by our staff.

Here's all you do:

Visit *www.facthound.com*

FactHound will fetch the best sites for you!

Index